ALBERT EINSTEIN

D1520327

BY ANNE SCHRAFF

Development: Kent Publishing Services, Inc.

Design and Production: Signature Design Group, Inc.

SADDLEBACK EDUCATIONAL PUBLISHING

Three Watson

Irvine, CA 92618-2767

Web site: www.sdlback.com

Photo Credits: pages 8, 42, 45, 61, Zuma Press;
page 24, KPA Photo Archive

ISBN-13: 978-1-59905-246-5

ISBN-10: 1-59905-246-6

eBook: 978-1-60291-607-4

Printed in China

1 2 3 4 5 6 10 09 08 07

TABLE of CONTENTS

In the 17th century, the scientist Sir Isaac Newton taught about space, matter, and time. He taught that space, matter, and time are separate from each other. Albert Einstein came along over 200 years later. He disagreed. He said all three are closely related, or relative to each other. They are connected. And they are connected in ways that can be hard to understand.

Einstein turned the world of science upside down with his theory of relativity. Einstein knew his ideas could play a part in the making of atomic bombs. He wanted them to be used as a force for peace. But he cried out in sorrow when atomic bombs took thousands of lives at the end of World War II.

Albert Einstein was born on Friday, March 14, 1879, in Ulm, Germany. The Einsteins were a middle class family. They had lived in southern Germany for over 300 years. Albert's father, Hermann, was a warm and **optimistic** man. He was an engineer whose many business ventures had failed. But he never stopped trying. Hermann Einstein married Pauline Koch, a gentle and intelligent young woman, in 1876. The Einsteins were Jews, but they did follow Hebrew religious practices. For example, they did not go to the **synagogue** or follow dietary laws.

Albert was the Einstein's first child. Pauline thought her baby son's head was an unusual shape. She worried that he might have mental problems. Her worry only increased when Albert was slow to learn to speak.

In 1880 the Einsteins moved to Munich, the capital of Bavaria and a center of industry. Albert's father hoped he'd have better luck there. In 1881 Albert's sister, Maja, was born. It was a happy home. The parents showered their two children with love. Grandparents, aunts, and uncles all interested in their well-being surrounded the children. Still, Albert was very quiet. Even at nine, he only spoke slowly and thoughtfully.

Albert Einstein was a curious young boy.

When Albert was very young, his father gave him a magnetic **compass**. The little boy was delighted and captivated by the compass. He kept studying it and turning it around and around. Albert also enjoyed doing jigsaw puzzles and building very high houses of cards. He liked to read, but he never chose light, funny books. He always wanted serious books that he could learn from.

As a young child, Albert was tutored at home. He had a very hot temper. One day, when he was frustrated, he picked up a chair and threw it at his tutor. The angry teacher fled, never to return. Albert learned to control his temper after that.

One day, Albert's parents took him to see a military parade. They thought he would enjoy seeing the marching soldiers and hearing the music. But Albert wept at the sight of the soldiers marching close together. They looked like a frightening monster with many arms and legs to the little boy. All his life, Albert would dislike the military.

Albert's mother was a talented pianist who passed on her love of music to her children. Albert loved to listen to his mother playing the piano.

Finally, it was time for Albert to attend regular school. His parents wanted to pick the best school they could find for their son. The nearest good school was a Catholic school. It had a fine academic record. The Einsteins did not care what religion was taught at the school. They only wanted their son to get a good education.

Albert Einstein enjoyed hearing the colorful Bible stories at the Catholic school. He was the only Jewish child in the whole school, but that was not a problem. The problem was that Albert just did not like school. He thought it had been better before with a tutor and his parents teaching him at home.

CHAPTER 2

Albert did not like the **discipline** of the classroom. He did not want to sit in one place. He did not want to do as he was told. He was rebellious and troublesome. He hated having to memorize. Albert preferred being alone, so he avoided the other children. He also disliked sports. He did not take part in any of the games.

Even though seven-year-old Albert did not like school, he worked hard. His report cards were excellent. But Albert always believed he learned the really important things at home. For example, his Uncle Jakob introduced him to algebra. He loved it from the beginning. Whenever the boy had some free time, he studied mathematics on his own. Albert also learned to play the violin at home. His love of music grew.

When he was ten years old, Albert was sent to Luitpold School, a secondary school. Again, he was very unhappy. He knew a lot more than the other students about mathematics and science. He was not popular with the other students. Albert began teaching himself **physics** and higher mathematics while studying the regular subjects at Luitpold.

To young Albert, school felt like the army. The teachers were like officers. He was told that he had to be like everybody else. He begged his father to move the family out of Germany.

Albert Einstein believed in pacifist ideals from a young age. He worried that he might be drafted into the German army. He believed that all conflicts between nations could be settled by peaceful compromise. He thought war was **barbaric**.

In 1894 when Albert was fifteen, his father failed in business again. Albert's father got a new job in Italy. The family packed up and left Germany. They took their daughter, Maja, with them. Since Albert had not yet graduated from high school, he was left behind. Albert was crushed. He had to live in a boarding house. He was miserable without his family.

After six months, Albert quit school and joined his family in Italy. His parents were upset that their son had left school without earning his high school diploma. It was impossible to enter most colleges without a high school diploma.

Albert loved Italy. He went to art galleries. He learned to sail. He climbed mountains. He listened to music. But his parents wanted him to earn a living in electrical engineering. He needed a university degree. Few universities enrolled students without their high school diploma. But his parents found one that required only that students pass an entrance test. It was called the Swiss Federal Polytechnic Institute. Albert scored well in math but didn't pass the general knowledge test.

The Institute sent Albert to school for a year in Aarau, a nearby town. There he prepared for the exam. Albert enjoyed school in Switzerland. He loved the land and the people. He felt free to study. He did not just have to memorize dates and facts. He took the test again, and this time he passed.

CHAPTER 3

Einstein planned to teach math and physics in high school. He began a four-year course at the Institute. He liked college better than high school. But he was still not a good student. He often cut classes. And he argued with his teachers when he disagreed with them.

Einstein enjoyed walking in the hills around the school. He liked to eat his meals in restaurants. In the evenings, he played music. Einstein and his friends each played an instrument. They would gather at someone's home or in a little coffee shop. Einstein played the violin and a young female student from Serbia, Mileva Maric, played the piano.

Young Albert took notice of the dark haired, dark-eyed Maric, and they became friends. But even though he enjoyed his friends, Einstein was most interested in self-study. He was constantly wondering about the rules of physics and trying to work out problems that interested him. When he and his friends went on sailboat rides, everyone relaxed. But Einstein wrote math problems and solutions on a notepad. His mind was always busy.

Einstein became a close friend of another student, Marcel Grossman. Einstein and Grossman and other friends spent hours discussing mathematical problems.

Although Einstein was recognized at the Institute as brilliant and gifted, he was unpopular with the professors. He was stubborn. He refused to listen to them and give them the respect they felt they deserved. In August 1900 Einstein graduated. Now twenty-one, he needed a job badly. He was living on an allowance from home, and his family was far from rich. Hermann Einstein never found a good enough position to give his family a worry free life. Albert Einstein wanted to be on his own and not add to the financial burdens of his family.

Einstein wrote letters to different schools asking for a position teaching mathematics. Since he had not made friends with his professors at the Institute, there were no helping hands reaching out to him. On his job applications, Einstein wrote that he had already published scientific articles in the *German Annals of Physics*. But after searching for a year he still had no job. He earned some money tutoring students in math and science. He took part time positions teaching when the regular teachers were ill. But he had no real job and no decent income.

In 1901 Albert Einstein became a citizen of Switzerland. He submitted a paper he had written to the University of Zurich in the hopes of getting his Ph.D. Such a degree would have increased his chances of finding work. His paper was rejected. Einstein was beginning to feel that the world was against him.

Down to his last few cents, Einstein got a long-term substitute teaching job at Winterthur, 17 miles north of Zurich. He taught mathematics to boys who were not interested at first. But Einstein discovered that he was able to gain their attention and teach them something. But that job ended and soon Einstein was so poor that he was cutting back on his meals and losing weight. He got another job tutoring boys, but he was fired when his employer disagreed with his methods.

Albert Einstein had almost given up hope of finding a good job. In 1902 his friend, Marcel Grossman, came to his rescue.

With the help of his friend, Marcel Grossman, Albert Einstein got a job in Bern, Switzerland, at the patent office as a third class examiner. His job was to be part of a technical team looking at new inventions and deciding if they deserved a patent. A patent is a document certifying that the invention worked and was original. Einstein loved to work with new inventions. He was like a child again, staring with wonder at that compass his father gave him. Einstein's skill and enthusiasm soon got him promoted to second class technical expert.

Mileva Maric was a physicist like Albert Einstein. She too had big dreams for her profession. She enjoyed discussing scientific theories with Einstein. She was intelligent enough to understand him. Originally from Greece with Serbian roots, she grew up in Hungary. Four years older than Einstein, she was bright, energetic, and quick. But Albert Einstein wanted a wife, not a partner in his work. He asked Maric to marry him. They were married in January 1903.

The young couple rented an apartment with a view of the Alps. Einstein was **pondering** the nature of light, concluding that it was made up of individual particles of energy, which he called photons. The scientific world at the time thought light was transmitted in waves.

Albert Einstein with his wife, Mileva Maric.

The Einstein's first son, Hans Albert, was born on May 14, 1904. Einstein was very happy as a father. He often wheeled his infant son down the street in a baby carriage. He even tried to help his wife with the household chores. Mileva Einstein was a perfectionist. Soon, she was taking care of the baby and the house while Einstein was writing scientific articles and thinking about atoms and **molecules**. At the time, no one knew for sure if atoms and molecules even existed.

Atoms and molecules are the smallest particles in nature. They are often invisible, even under a microscope. Einstein wanted to prove that these invisible particles behaved just like larger, visible particles. He noticed that larger particles moved around when in a liquid. He thought they were being hit by smaller, invisible particles. The only way to prove his theory was through mathematics.

The motion of particles was called Brownian Motion. Einstein published an article, "On the Movement of Small Particles," in 1905. He proved the existence of molecules and their motion. For this discovery, Albert Einstein was awarded a Doctor of Philosophy degree from the University of Zurich.

1905 was an incredible year for Einstein. It came to be called a "Wonderful Year." He published a number of research papers that changed science forever. While working full time at the patent office, he produced revolutionary theories about space, matter, and time.

Einstein turned his attention to the study of light. The speed of light had been **verified** as 186,000 miles a second. Now Einstein concluded that the speed of light in free space was the only fixed thing in the universe. Everything else is relative. This was called his "Theory of Relativity."

According to Einstein, time is variable. For example, if someone walked beside a man bouncing a ball, the path of the ball would look straight up and down. But if you stood still, and the man walked past you bouncing the ball, the ball would appear to move diagonally up and down. So it would seem as if the ball went a longer distance in the same amount of time. The idea of time and space, then, depended on the observer and where he was.

Another example is a sailor raising a flag on a ship. To the sailor standing at the base of the flagpole, the flag moves straight up. But to an observer on shore, the flag moves forward and up at the same time. Time and space are relative. They depend on the observer's frame of reference.

Einstein published his article on special relativity in the *Annals of Physics*. When other scientists read it, some were upset. They thought this twenty-six-year-old upstart was tampering with Isaac Newton's fixed laws. Others, however, knew Einstein's insights were important. They increased our understanding of the universe.

CHAPTER 5

Albert Einstein then began to think about energy and matter. Einstein said they are different forms of the same thing. His idea was that if matter moved fast enough, it became energy. If energy was slowed down, it became matter. He introduced a mathematical equation to prove this theory: $E = mc^2$. "E" stands for energy, "m" stands for mass, and "c^2" stands for the speed of light multiplied by itself. The equation says that there is a huge amount of energy tied up in even a small amount of matter. For the first time, someone explained how the sun could go on giving off light for billions of years without cooling off.

Albert Einstein came up with these amazing ideas when he was still a clerk at the patent office. His friends told him that with his knowledge, he should be a university professor. But Einstein feared having teaching responsibilities. He thought teaching would take too much time from his research.

Einstein was receiving invitations to lecture at universities. Mileva Einstein was hoping for a better career for her husband. Einstein enjoyed work at the patent office. But he wondered if he would always be happy looking at new inventions.

In 1909 Albert Einstein became a professor of physics at the University of Zurich. Albert and Mileva Einstein fell in love with Zurich. It was a happy time for the family. Albert Einstein enjoyed playing games and telling stories to his five-year-old son. Albert and Mileva often attended the opera and the theatre. On July 28, 1910, the Einstein's second son was born. Eduard was given the pet nickname of "Tete." Unlike the robust Hans, Eduard was a **frail** child.

With the birth of a second child, Mileva Einstein believed the family needed more money. Einstein added more lectures. He began thinking about the problems of gravity. In 1911 Einstein was offered a higher salary to teach at the University of Prague. Soon, Albert Einstein's fame spread. He was invited to meetings with world famous scientists. Then Einstein was offered three jobs, director of physics at the **prestigious** Kaiser Wilhelm Institute, membership in the Prussian Academy of Science, and professor at the University of Berlin.

News that the family might be moving to Germany made Mileva Einstein very unhappy. Einstein accepted the new jobs. Mileva Einstein and her two sons continued to live in Switzerland. The marriage was over. She had been unhappy for a long time because her own career as a physicist never developed. She was frustrated with her husband's personality.

Mileva Einstein began a new life as a divorcée and single mother with two young boys. Albert Einstein supported his family financially. He made regular trips to Switzerland to see his sons. But he was very lonely living alone in Berlin.

To relieve his loneliness, Einstein often visited his Uncle Rudolf who lived in Berlin. Rudolf Einstein's daughter, Elsa, lived there as well with her two daughters, Margot and Ilse. Albert Einstein and Elsa Einstein were cousins. They had often played together as children. He felt very comfortable with her. He liked the two girls, too. When Albert played the violin and Elsa played the piano, the girls were charmed.

Einstein found he liked living in Berlin. The people were friendlier than he expected. He spent much of his time studying gravity. He also spent pleasant hours with Elsa and her daughters. Like Einstein, Elsa was also divorced. She scolded Albert for not taking better care of himself. He seemed much too thin.

Unlike Mileva, Elsa was not a brilliant woman. She was simple, kind, and down to earth. Little by little, she became an important part of Albert Einstein's life.

But another dark cloud was looming over the life of Einstein and all of Europe. In 1914 it appeared that the world would soon be going to war.

CHAPTER 6

Albert Einstein hated war. He was a pacifist. He joined with other scientists in pleading with Europeans to start a league dedicated to peace. Einstein began to promote peace, tolerance, and justice. He was horrified by the thought of Europe being torn apart by war. But by the end of the summer of 1914, full-scale war raged. Injuries and death mounted on both sides. Einstein saw it as senseless evil.

Einstein still worked on his new ideas about space, matter, and time. He wanted to show how gravity fit with his ideas. After eight years of work, he concluded that gravity was the product of space distorted by the presence of matter. In 1916 Einstein published his ideas as the "General Theory of Relativity." This has been called his most important achievement.

Einstein said that a beam of light would be bent by gravity as it passed a star. The gravity of the star would cause the light beam to curve. In 1919 Einstein"s theory was tested. British astronomers photographed stars during a total eclipse of the sun. The photographs were compared with pictures of the same stars when the sun was far off. The different positions of the stars on the two different photographs proved that the sun deflects starlight.

Einstein's general theory of relativity helped explain such things as the curved shape of the universe. It also explained why the universe is expanding, what black holes are, and the "**big bang**" theory of how the universe began.

In 1919 five months after his divorce to Mileva Einstein was final, Albert Einstein married Elsa Einstein Lowenthal. Einstein legally adopted Elsa's two daughters. He enjoyed them **immensely**. Once again, Albert Einstein had a happy home. But he continued to work hard. Elsa tenderly cared for him when he was sick.

Einstein spent a lot of time reading philosophy and listening to music. He worked to discover what is called a unified field theory. Einstein sought to discover a single law that explains how all natural forces work.

Einstein continued to see his sons. In 1920 he met fifteen-year-old Hans in Italy. They hiked for several days and Einstein shared fatherly advice.

In 1920 Albert Einstein was the subject of much publicity and admiration. But in Germany, his work was sometimes criticized. Anti-semitism was a terrible problem in Germany. After the end of World War I, it flared with increased energy. Some Germans, **embittered** by the fact that they lost World War I, blamed the Jews. They also blamed the Jews for terrible unemployment and inflation in Germany. Einstein's theories were ridiculed as "Jewish physics."

In Germany, there was a small group of angry Germans promoting the idea that only pure "**Aryan**" Germans were worthy human beings. All non-Aryans, especially Jews, were belittled. The leader of this violent movement was a former house painter named Adolf Hitler. At that time, hardly anyone suspected the role Hitler would play in the future. But Einstein and other thoughtful men were disgusted and alarmed.

CHAPTER 7

In 1921 Chaim Weizmann, a chemistry professor and leader of the **Zionist movement** asked for Einstein's help in establishing Hebrew University in Palestine. The Zionists wanted to create a homeland for Jewish people. Einstein accompanied Weizmann on a trip to the United States. The Einsteins arrived in New York in April. Reporters crowded about to interview him.

Albert Einstein was invited to the White House to meet President Franklin Roosevelt. The family was greeted wherever they went with warmth and good will.

Columbia University gave him a medal and offered him a job. Einstein raised millions of dollars for Hebrew University.

Einstein gave a series of lectures at Princeton University. His lectures on the theory of relativity were delivered in German. An American professor then gave the same lecture in English. The lectures were published in a book, *The Meaning of Relativity.* Princeton gave him an honorary degree.

After the U.S. trip, Einstein traveled the world. He met with scientists and gave lectures. During a trip to Japan, he learned that he won the Nobel Prize in physics.

Einstein demonstrates his formulas on a blackboard during a lecture.

He was also awarded membership into all of the leading scientific academies.

Meanwhile, trouble was brewing in Germany. The Nazi Party was gaining in popularity. Even as his fame was growing around the world, Einstein's belief in peace and a unified Europe was not popular at home. Prejudice against Jews made Germany a dangerous place for the Einstein family. Friends begged them to leave the troubled country.

In 1933 the Einsteins moved permanently to the United States. Einstein was invited to become a professor at Princeton University in New Jersey. Einstein's sister, Maja, also came to the United States. Hans Einstein, his son, found work in the United States as an engineer.

The magnificent **campus** of Princeton University awed Albert Einstein. When he was asked how he wanted his office furnished, he asked for a desk, a chair, and a wastebasket where he could throw his mistakes.

The Einsteins were touched by the kindness of ordinary people. Children approached him everywhere he went. They knew who he was. On Christmas Eve, groups of boys and girls sang carols for the Einsteins. Albert Einstein rushed outside and asked the children if he could get his violin and join them as they made the rounds of the neighborhood. Wearing a leather jacket and stocking cap and playing his violin, Einstein became a caroler that night.

Albert Einstein decided to become a citizen of the United States.

*Albert Einstein taking part in a ceremony,
making him a citizen of the United States.*

CHAPTER 8

Albert Einstein continued to believe in **pacifism**, but the actions of Adolf Hitler were changing his mind. He was beginning to fear that nothing but military force would stop Hitler.

In the mid-1930s, the Einsteins lived a simple life. They had no car and few luxuries. Einstein gained all the joy he needed listening to music and walking in the woods. In 1936 Elsa Einstein became pale and tired. She refused to go to the hospital and nurses cared for her at home. Finally, she grew so ill that Albert Einstein had to hospitalize her. In December 1936 Elsa Einstein died.

Einstein was devastated by the loss of his wife. His loneliness was eased when his stepdaughter, Margot, came to live with him. Einstein and a colleague wrote a book, *Evolution of Physics,* which was published in 1937.

Late in 1939 some Hungarian physicists with alarming news visited Albert Einstein. They believed Adolf Hitler's scientists were close to producing an atomic bomb. They urged Einstein to use his great prestige to convince President Roosevelt to immediately begin work on an American atomic bomb.

Einstein was horrified about urging the development of such a terrible weapon. But he feared that if Hitler developed the bomb first, humanity would be in peril. So he wrote the letter to President Roosevelt describing how an atomic bomb could be produced. President Roosevelt set American scientists to work on the project.

In October 1940 Albert Einstein took the oath of American citizenship. In December 1941 the United States was attacked by Japan at Pearl Harbor, and Einstein's adopted country was fighting for its life. Einstein did everything he could for the war effort. He urged Americans to buy **war bonds,** and he gave advice to the scientists working on the **Manhattan Project** to build the atomic bomb.

As the war raged on with mounting **casualties**, Einstein mourned. Germany surrendered in May 1945, but the United States was still fighting Japan. Then, in the summer of 1945, Albert Einstein learned of the bombing of Hiroshima, Japan. He was told that over sixty thousand people had died in an atomic blast. Many more would die of radiation sickness.

Days later, another atomic bomb was dropped on Nagasaki, Japan. About forty thousand lives were lost. Japan surrendered quickly, ending World War II, but Albert Einstein was heartsick. He said if he had known the atomic bomb would be used in this way by the United States he never would have written to President Roosevelt urging atomic research. Einstein tried to believe that he was not directly responsible for the bomb. But for Einstein, the devoted pacifist, the horrors of Hiroshima and Nagasaki haunted him. He had always hated war. This was war at its absolute worst.

Einstein looked for a way to turn the pain he was feeling into something useful. He resolved to work **diligently** for peace so never again would atomic bombs be dropped on a city. He joined with other physicists to ask for a world government with a military force that would make sure World War III would never happen.

After World War II, the Cold War began between the non-communist world of the United States and her allies and the **communist** world of Russia and her allies. There was great fear of communism throughout the United

States. Einstein's campaign for peace led some to believe he was leaning toward communism.

Einstein was sorry that he was misunderstood. But he felt compelled to work for peace while he was still working on scientific problems.

C H A P T E R 9

Albert Einstein had received degrees from universities all over the world. He had so many medals and honors that he lost count. The Einstein Institute of Mathematics at the Hebrew University of Jerusalem was named for him. Albert Einstein was thought to be one of the most important men in the world.

Einstein continued to think and kept his pad and pencil near for mathematical equations. Einstein always refused to believe that anything in the universe happens purely by chance. He believed that laws govern everything, and he continued to struggle to find those laws.

Einstein campaigned on for world government and for a ban on atomic weapons. He felt sure that atomic weapons posed a threat to the human race.

In 1952 Einstein's old friend and fellow scientist, Chaim Weizmann, the first president of Israel, died. To his astonishment, Einstein was offered Weizmann's job as president of Israel. Some Israelis believed that having Einstein as their president would increase the influence of the new nation. Einstein refused. He could not imagine himself as a politician.

Now seventy-three, Einstein was often caught up in sadness. Many of his old friends had died. He still missed Elsa, his wife. He worried about the health of his beloved stepdaughter, Margot.

Albert Einstein worried about what he saw as moral decay in society. He loved science, but he believed that the struggle for justice and truth was more important than anything else. He said that people can find meaning in life only by promoting good in society.

In his old age, Einstein enjoyed the company of his wire-haired terrier, Chico, and young people. Children often joined him on walks, peppering him with questions. Like the children, Einstein continued to be delighted by the wonders of nature.

Einstein greatly admired the spiritual leader of India, Mahatma Gandhi. Gandhi, a tireless **advocate** of non-violence, had done so much for humanity. Gandhi, like Einstein, was a pacifist.

March 14, 1954 was Albert Einstein's seventy-fifth birthday. Tributes poured in from around the world. When he heard the voices of praise, Einstein asked what he had done to deserve this.

A young student asked Einstein what he believed in, and he answered the brotherhood of man. Einstein described science without religion as lame, and religion without science as blind.

CHAPTER 10

Half a dozen years earlier, Albert Einstein found out he had a serious medical condition—a weak spot in one of his arteries. Einstein ignored this, and in April 1955 he became seriously ill with stomach pain, often a **symptom** of heart trouble. The family doctor sent for specialists who suggested surgery might be necessary. Einstein refused an operation saying he was too old. But he did agree to enter Princeton Hospital for a few days.

Albert Einstein referred to death as "the old debt" which all people must pay. He felt his time to pay the debt was close, but he did not want to stay in the hospital. When his son, Hans, came from California, Einstein assured him he was feeling better.

Even while he lay in his hospital bed, Einstein asked that his latest pages of mathematical equations be brought to him so he might add something.

In the very early hours of the morning of April 18, 1955, Einstein began mumbling in German. The nurse who was with him did not understand German so she could not tell anyone what Einstein's last words were. He died before the next day dawned. The weakened artery had apparently burst.

Einstein had known for some time that he was dying and he made plans for it. He wanted no funeral, no grave, and no monument. Albert Einstein was not a religious man. He believed the universe was so awesome that it had to have been created by a supreme intelligence. His name for this creator was "the old gentleman."

Einstein wanted his body cremated with the ashes disposed of secretly. He felt his work was the important thing about his life, and he did not want his earthly remains to be the center of attention.

He did permit his brain to be removed during an **autopsy**. Scientists wanted to discover if there was anything unusual about the brain of a genius. They did find that the part of Einstein's brain associated with mathematical reasoning, the inferior parietal, was fifteen percent wider on both sides than normal.

Albert Einstein was considered to be one of the world's rare geniuses, as Isaac Newton was in his time.

Fame and popularity meant nothing to Einstein. In fact, they often distressed him. He had little use for wealth or material goods. He continued to be amazed that people needed so many things to make them happy. He was a humble, patient, and dedicated man. His joy was derived from observing nature and finding scientific truths.

Time magazine voted Albert Einstein the person who made the most important contributions to the 20th century. Einstein himself would not have agreed. He always mourned the victims of the atomic bomb and feared a future world war that might destroy the world he loved so much. In the end, Albert Einstein's determination to work for human brotherhood and world peace was perhaps as important as his revolutionary ideas about space, matter, and time.

*Albert Einstein is regarded by many
as the most important scientist of the
20th century and the greatest physicist
of all time.*

BIBLIOGRAPHY

Abraham, Carolyn. *Possessing Genius: The Bizarre Journey of Einstein's Brain.* New York: St. Martin's Press, 2002.

Kaku, Michio. *Albert Einstein: How Albert Einstein's Vision Transformed Our Understanding of Time and Space.* New York: W.W. Norton, 2004.

Overbye, Dennis. *Einstein in Love: A Scientific Romance.* New York: Viking, 2000.

GLOSSARY

advocate: someone who supports or speaks in favor of something

Aryan: in Nazi ideology, a Caucasian, non-semitic person considered to be superior to others because of race

autopsy: a medical examination of a dead body in order to determine the cause or circumstances of death

barbaric: uncivilized , primitive, unusually cruel

Big Bang: a theory of the origin of the universe that says the universe developed out of the explosion of a single extremely dense mass of matter

campus: the area of land that contains the buildings and grounds of a university or college

casualties: people who are seriously injured or killed during combat or in an accident

communist: a supporter of communism, a system of government in which the state controls wealth, property, and the economy

compass: a device for finding directions that uses a magnetized pointer that indicates north

diligently: industriously

discipline: the ability to act in a controlled and orderly manner

embittered: disillusioned, resentful

frail: weak, flimsy

immensely: to a very large extent or degree

Manhattan Project: a project funded by the U.S. government during World War II to develop the first atomic bomb

molecule: the smallest part of a substance consisting of a single set of atoms

optimistic: expressing a cheerful and positive attitude about the future

pacifism: a belief that violent ways of resolving disputes are unacceptable frequently because of religious or moral principles

physics: the science of matter, energy, force, and motion

pondering: thinking about, meditating on

prestigious: important, prominent, distinguished

symptom: indication, evidence

synagogue: the place of worship for a Jewish congregation

verified: confirmed, proved

war bonds: a type of savings bond issued by a government to finance a war

Zionist movement: the political and religious movement that advocated for a homeland for the Jewish people in the biblical land of Israel

INDEX